IMAGES
of America

FORT ABRAHAM LINCOLN

On the Cover: Lt. Col. George Armstrong Custer and his inner circle of officers and friends are standing in front of Custer's first residence at Fort Abraham Lincoln. In February 1874, this residence burned down. A second was built, which informed the reconstructed house that resides at Fort Abraham Lincoln State Park today. Custer is third from left in this photograph. Custer indeed understood the power of images and frequently had his photograph taken during his tenure and final years at Fort Abraham Lincoln. (Denver Public Library.)

IMAGES
of America

FORT ABRAHAM LINCOLN

Aaron L. Barth

ARCADIA
PUBLISHING

ISBN 978-1-4671-2686-1

Published by Arcadia Publishing
Charleston, South Carolina

Printed in the United States of America

Library of Congress Control Number: 2017956370

For all general information, please contact Arcadia Publishing:
Telephone 843-853-2070
Fax 843-853-0044
E-mail sales@arcadiapublishing.com
For customer service and orders:
Toll-Free 1-888-313-2665

Visit us on the Internet at www.arcadiapublishing.com

Contents

Acknowledgments

This volume pulls together photographs from the archives of the State Historical Society of North Dakota (SHSND) at Bismarck; North Dakota State University (NDSU) at Fargo; the National Park Service Little Bighorn National Monument (NPS) in Crow Agency, Montana; the South Dakota State Historical Society (SDSHS) in Pierre; the Minnesota State Historical Society (MSHS) in St. Paul; the Denver Public Library (DPL); and the National Archives and Records Administration (NARA).

Introduction

Fort Abraham Lincoln State Park holds multiple layers of history from several cultures within today's park boundaries. There are four periods when construction projects changed the look and feel of the landscape.

One of the earliest was the original establishment of the Mandan "earthlodge" village, sometimes referred to as "On-A-Slant," or more traditionally referred to as Miti-nemak-henuk, or "Watchman's Village." This infrastructure period started around 1550 and was one of several interconnected villages up and down the Missouri River. This period marked the rise of the Mandan Indians, and this site was one of several confederations of Mandan Villages.

The nearby location of the Heart River also served as the marker of the Húŋkpapȟa Lakȟóta and Iháŋktȟuŋwaŋna Dakȟóta (Yanktonai), members of what in the 19th century was known as the Great Sioux Nation, or what traditionally was called the Očhéthi Šakówiŋ. These tribes established this water boundary in the 1803 Battle of Heart River after years of intertribal conflict with the Mandan.

The Mandan villages were a center of intertribal North American trade for hundreds of years. They acquired the horse from their southern neighbors, the Cheyenne, sometime around 1700. In 1781, a devastating smallpox epidemic struck the Mandan forcing the survivors to abandon their homeland and move north up the Missouri River to the confluence of the Knife River. Miti-nemak-henuk village was the childhood home of the Mandan civil chief Shehek Shote, White Wolf (also known as Sheheke, or White Coyote), who met with Pres. Thomas Jefferson. The village was partially reconstructed by the Civilian Conservation Corps (CCC) in the 1930s and was renamed Miti-bawa-esh, or On-A-Slant.

Just after Pres. Thomas Jefferson completed the Louisiana Purchase land sale with Napoleon and France, the Corps of Discovery was ordered on an expeditionary ascent up the Missouri River. Lewis and Clark passed by and overnighted about a mile north of the abandoned Mandan village on October 20, 1804. A marker overlooks the Missouri and Heart River confluence to memorialize the Corps' visit. A medallion in front of the CCC museum demarcates the Corps of Discovery Bicentennial with the text "Peace and Friendship."

At least one oral tradition connected with the local landscape concerns a story between the Mandan and Teton nations. It is the story of a woman who turned to stone. Long ago, the Thítȟuŋwaŋ (the literal translation is "Dwellers on the Plains," today known as Teton) came to trade, and one man wanted to take a Mandan woman to be his wife. He took her moccasins so that she would be more inclined not to run away from him, but her resolve was stronger than he knew and she left him with nothing on her feet. About halfway up today's hill that leads to Fort McKeen, the Mandan woman turned to stone—not out of divine punishment, but that future Mandan women remembered her resolve to return to her people, and her refusal to give up her heritage. Cottonwood trees grew in her footsteps. The trees were eventually cut down, leaving only a few, which were transplanted by soldiers to the front of the officer quarters of Fort McKeen.

The second phase of infrastructure arrived with the US military and the establishment of Fort McKeen in June 1872 and Fort Abraham Lincoln in November of that same year. Hundreds of railroad carloads of materials went into this infrastructure build out.

The original Fort Abraham Lincoln military reservation boundary measured about 23 miles square. Within this boundary ran the Little Heart River to the south, and extended as far as Little Heart Butte, a plateau about 13 miles south and west of Fort Abraham Lincoln.

In the late winter, or spring, of 1875, Itómağažu (Rain-in-the-Face), a prominent Húŋkpapȟa chieftain, made a daring escape from the fort's guardhouse after three months of incarceration. Rain was arrested by Capt. Tom Custer for the murder of railroad personnel in 1873 in Yellowstone country. One report says he escaped, but his own account says that he was released by a sympathetic guard, an old holdover from the fur trader era.

In May 1875, Lieutenant Colonel Custer hosted the Treaty of Fort Abraham Lincoln, which was the federal government's attempt to bring peace between several tribes; some of whom had been at war for several generations. As soon as the treaty concluded, the tribes resumed their intertribal conflicts.

Fort Abraham Lincoln State Park bears the distinction of being named after the shortest occupation of all, Fort Abraham Lincoln (1873–1890). During Ulysses S. Grant's presidential tenure in Washington, DC, this fort was named in honor and memoriam of the assassinated Pres. Abraham Lincoln. The fort encompassed six companies of cavalry, two companies of infantry, and a detachment of US Indian Scouts drawn from the Santee, Arikara, Crow, and Blackfoot as well as an African American. Fort Abraham Lincoln is best known for being the last command of Lt. Col. George Custer and the starting point of the Centennial Campaign of 1876, which concluded at the Battle of the Little Bighorn.

Following the Battle of the Little Bighorn, Fort Abraham Lincoln became a prison camp for members of the Northern Cheyenne after Col. Nelson Miles employed a detachment of US Indian Scouts from the Northern Cheyenne on his campaign against the Nez Perce. Following the conflict at Bear's Paw Mountain, Miles captured the weary Nez Perce and brought them to Fort Abraham Lincoln in October 1877 for processing before they were shipped off to Indian Territory. At least 10 Nez Perce died at Fort Abraham Lincoln.

Four conflicts lie within the old Fort Abraham Lincoln military reservation: an Indian Wars conflict where Gen. Henry Sibley followed the Húŋkpapȟa Lakȟóta, Santee, and Iháŋktȟuŋwaŋna Dakȟóta to the Missouri River between the Heart River and Apple Creek and concluded in a three-day conflict in July 1863; a "wood cutter" fight on the north side of Fort McKeen between the Húŋkpapȟa and the 17th Infantry in the summer of 1872; a skirmish between the US Indian Scouts and the Húŋkpapȟa Lakȟóta in 1873 south of the fort along Little Heart Creek; and a three-day long gunfight between the US Indian Scouts and Húŋkpapȟa Lakȟóta in 1874, at Little Heart Butte. These conflicts happened beyond the boundaries of today's Fort Abraham Lincoln State Park boundaries. They are important to note, though, as today's park represents the infrastructural hub by which the United States colonized the continental interior, first through the system of territories and forts, and then with settlers and formal statehood. This system is not without controversy, both then and today, as the federal government is long known for having made and broken innumerable treaties with the indigenous nations in this area and throughout the nation. President Roosevelt recognized the importance of Fort Abraham Lincoln and made sure this federal fort was gifted to the state of North Dakota in 1907. Like many forts, it transitioned into a place for heritage recreation.

The third and fourth heavy infrastructure lifts arrived to memorialize, remember and reflect on the first two. In the 1930s, the Civilian Conservation Corps built a museum, administration and concessions building, shelters, parking lots, and bridges in WPA Rustic architectural style. They also rebuilt several earth lodges under the instruction of the Mandan woman named Scattered Corn. The CCC also built infantry post blockhouses, the infantry fortification wall, and roughly marked the corners of the old Fort Abraham Lincoln building locations. In the 1930s, the CCC noted that it would be too much of a maintenance burden to rebuild every structure the way it was in the 1870s, so they decided to limit the amount of construction.

A half century later, in the 1980s, area volunteers and professionals established the 501(c)3 non-profit Fort Abraham Lincoln Foundation (FALF). In a collaborative coordinated effort, FALF and local enthusiasts raised funds to rebuild Lt. Col. George Armstrong Custer's final and last commanding officer's quarters. Then, throughout the 1990s, through private and public funding, FALF helped coordinate the reconstruction of the buildings at Fort Abraham Lincoln and earthlodges at On-A-Slant Village. It did not stop there. FALF also helped with the heavy lift of updating the museum exhibits within the 1930s CCC museum and leveraging funding to develop a world class interpretive program.

Mounds and anvil stones rest at the park's highest point and share the site of the infantry's old Fort McKeen. These mounds have been identified by archaeologists as originating from the Late Woodland Period, from 500 to 1000 CE. The mouth of the Heart River was once the southernmost boundary of the Heart River phase, a period lasting from about 1500 to 1781.

Fort Abraham Lincoln has nationally important history from several eras. This village site was one of the several sites that made up the Mandan confederation, a trading hub that had continental reach. Its proximity to the Heart River also situates it as a village at the heart of the Mandan origin story. The only North Dakotans that President Thomas Jefferson had the privilege to meet are from On-A-Slant Village. Fort Abraham Lincoln is the final fort that Lt. Col. George Armstrong Custer departed from on the fateful journey to the Battle of Little Bighorn/Greasy Grass during the nation's centennial in 1876. And this fort housed the Nez Perce as POWs in the late 1870s. The park's history recalls Mandan ancestry, continental trade, and represents failed Indian policies of the post–Civil War 19th century. Like many military forts on the Great Plains and throughout the American West, Fort Abraham Lincoln was turned over to a public agency for heritage and recreational purposes. It has indeed benefitted the public in this capacity for decades and generations.

Fort Abraham Lincoln State Park is overseen and managed by the North Dakota Department of Parks and Recreation.

—Dakota Goodhouse, Ozúye Núŋpa (Two Wars)

One

Fort Abraham Lincoln to 1891

This is an overview of Fort Abraham Lincoln photographed in the winter. The view is from Fort McKeen, and the camera faces to the south-southeast. The photographer was D.F. Barry. From 1989 to the present, the Fort Abraham Lincoln Foundation, along with countless volunteers, rebuilt a handful of buildings within this photograph. This includes the commanding officer's quarters, the commissary, one of two granaries, one of three infantry barracks, and a cavalry stable. (DPL.)

This overview of Fort Abraham Lincoln looks to the south-southeast, with the Missouri River winding into the distance. The Missouri River was the natural steamboat highway connecting Fort Abraham Lincoln to urban centers such as St. Louis down river. (SHSND.)

This is a winter photograph of "officer's row," with the commissary building at center right. D.F. Barry is the photographer. A horse and sleigh are also visible, as is an unidentified onlooker. The Fort Abraham Lincoln Foundation reconstructed the commissary in the 1990s. While today's commissary has modern conveniences, the exterior look keeps with the historical accuracy of the 1870s. (DPL.)

This photograph of the commanding officer's quarters was taken sometime after 1876. Additions to the original include the sun porch on the southeast corner and the room that extends out from the south (left) elevation. (DPL.)

Pictured above is another winter overview of Fort Abraham Lincoln, with smoke rising from the various chimneys. As it concerns late-19th-century architecture from this period, in the northern climates, chimneys tended to be located central in the buildings to maximize heat transfer. In locations closer to the equator, chimneys were often located on an exterior wall. (NPS.)

In this overview of Fort Abraham Lincoln, white canvas tent villages surrounding the fort are visible. These tent villages represented the civilian contingent of forts, including teams of laundresses. As the name suggests, laundresses would launder the uniforms of officers and soldiers. (NPS.)

On the back of this photograph, handwriting reads, "Our picnic camp, Heart River, Dakota [Territory]." Wagon wheel tracks are visible in the bottom center of the image. The Heart River empties into the Missouri River just to the northeast of historic Fort Abraham Lincoln. The "Heart" in this Heart River is the namesake of Elizabeth Fenn's 2015 Pulitzer Prize–winning history, *Encounters at the Heart of the World: A History of the Mandan People* (Hill & Wang). (NPS.)

The first commanding officer's quarters at Fort Abraham Lincoln, this photograph was taken sometime prior to February 1874. Lieutenant Colonel Custer sits on the railing, with a handful of officers and spouses on the front steps. In *Custer in Photographs,* (Garryowen, Montana: Custer Battlefield Museum Publishing, 2001), D. Mark Katz identifies the photographer as Orlando S. Goff, and individuals in the photograph from left as Lieutenant Colonel Custer, Margaret C. Calhoun, Lt. James Calhoun, Annie Yates, Agnes Bates, Elizabeth Bacon Custer, and Capt. William Thompson. (NPS.)

This photograph shows the parlor room within the commanding officer's quarters. The dining room is visible at center right in the image. The parlor room was a room for conversation, entertaining, music and singing. Written on this photograph is "1875," so decoration, plants, accoutrements, piano, and harp would have been those of Elizabeth and George Custer. (NPS.)

Taken in 1875, this is a photograph of the commanding officer's quarters by photographer Orlando S. Goff. Individuals identified from left to right by Elizabeth Custer are Leonard Swett, W.C. Curtis, Elizabeth B. Custer, Lt. James Calhoun, Emma Wadsworth, Lt. Col. George A. Custer, 1st Lt. Thomas W. Custer, Margaret Custer Calhoun, 2nd Lt. Richard E. Thompson, Nellie Wadsworth, and an unidentified soldier. (NPS.)

This is an overview of officer's row within Fort Abraham Lincoln. This view is pointed to the east-northeast. Ladders are present near some of the residences for construction and maintenance. The original of this image is on file with the Minnesota State Historical Society in St. Paul. Minnesota State Historical Society. (MSHS.)

Above is a photograph of the hospital at Fort Abraham Lincoln. This hospital was located toward the northern portion of the fort. (SHSND.)

This is a photograph of the interior of Lieutenant Colonel Custer's office within the commanding officer's quarters at Fort Abraham Lincoln. Hanging from the wall is a picture of Gen. George B. McClellan, with whom Custer served as an aide during the Civil War. It is also said that Custer consumed one raw onion per day, something he picked up from General McClellan during the Civil War. (SHSND.)

Individuals identified within this 1875 photograph include Edith Leisure (left), H.R. Porter (third from left), Jimmie Raymond (second from left), Tom Winston (sixth from left, standing), "Pet" Wilson (fifth from left), and Jack Leisure (tenth from left, sitting). (SHSND.)

This is one of the few (if only) photographs of the morgue at Fort Abraham Lincoln. Death did not always come through formal military skirmishes or battles. Inadequate nutrition contributed to illness and, in some cases, the death of soldiers. Death also came by way of fights between soldiers and civilians. In other cases, soldiers crossing the Missouri River in the winter sometimes fell through the ice. (SHSND.)

This quartermaster house was one of the last structures to be removed after the decommissioning of Fort Abraham Lincoln. Quartermasters tended to be senior soldiers charged with organizing and distributing supplies and provisions. Quartermaster employees included numerous teamsters needed to drive the horses and mules that supplied the armies. The industrial scale of armies in the second half of the 19th century necessitated this organization and scale. (SHSND.)

The building above was identified by the State Historical Society of North Dakota as "Goodings Store Fort Abraham Lincoln." (SHSND.)

The building seen here was identified by the State Historical Society of North Dakota as the commissary, Fort Abraham Lincoln. The commissary was a place that housed food and supplies for sale to personnel and workers at Fort Abraham Lincoln. (SHSND.)

This is a photograph of one of the three infantry barracks at Fort Abraham Lincoln. While the 7th Cavalry tended to take up a good deal of popular attention, several companies of infantry were also stationed at the fort. Throughout the 1990s, the Fort Abraham Lincoln Foundation—through massive local volunteer efforts, a board of directors, coordination with North Dakota's DC delegation and staff—helped rebuild two of the infantry barracks, and outfit them in a way that appears similar to 1875. (SHSND.)

This June 1877 photograph of "officer's row" at Fort Abraham Lincoln was taken by Frank Jay Haynes (1853–1921), the official Northern Pacific Railroad photographer who extensively documented the earliest years of Fort Abraham Lincoln and the city of Bismarck, Dakota Territory. Haynes is also known for photographing Deadwood and Yellowstone National Park. Throughout the 1980s, a collaborative of local volunteers, enthusiasts, and local corporate citizens dedicated resources to start and sustain the Fort Abraham Lincoln Foundation. Through this effort, the collaboration led to the reconstruction of the commanding officer's quarters in 1989. As of 2017, the commanding officer's quarters —also known as the Custer House—is the only building on officer's row to have been reconstructed. (SHSND.)

Visible in the distance within this 1876 photographic overview of Fort Abraham Lincoln is a collection of tents in the upper right hand corner of the photo. Buildings within this 1876 photograph reconstructed today include the commanding officer's quarters, the commissary, the granary, one infantry barracks, and one cavalry stable. (SHSND.)

This photograph of the fort from the Missouri River faces west toward the infantry barracks. The photographer is W.H. DeGraff, of Washburn, North Dakota. This is one of the few photographs of Fort Abraham Lincoln that appears to have been taken from the river. (SHSND.)

This 1882 image of Fort Abraham Lincoln was taken when the Northern Pacific Railroad (NPRR) bridge crossing was under construction that spanned the Missouri River at Bismarck-Mandan. Fort Abraham Lincoln was originally established to protect NPRR construction and workers. The NPRR signaled the arrival of the industrial revolution to the northern Plains. General George B. Dandy oversaw the original 1873 construction of the fort. Construction required up to 200 laborers and 700 railroad car loads of supplies. (SHSND.)

Two

PEOPLE TO 1891

Here, the infantry pose next to a Gatling gun and fortified wall. The letter "D" is distinguishable on two of the soldier's kepis, the soldier caps with round flat tops and a brim. While the 7th Cavalry dominated the popular image of Fort Abraham Lincoln, infantry companies were also stationed at the fort. Used at Fort Abraham Lincoln and by colonizing forces, including Great Britain, the Gatling gun represented the industrial mechanization of warfare throughout the world. (DPL.)

The infantry poses with a Gatling gun on the parade grounds, with officer's row in the background. Gatling guns operated by a hand-crank mechanism, with six barrels revolving around the central shaft. The Gatling gun eventually forced militaries to reconsider strategies of war and develop counter technologies and strategies. (SHSND.)

This photograph shows the infantry at attention on the parade grounds with infantry barracks behind them. The US War Department issued infantry rifles that were far longer in length than cavalry rifles. Infantry rifles also allowed for fixed bayonets. Minnesota State Historical Society.

The photograph shows a Gatling gun, infantry, and Fort McKeen blockhouses and barracks visible in the background. Photographer F. Jay Haynes took this as the official photographer of the Northern Pacific Railroad. Fort McKeen and Fort Abraham Lincoln were established as military outposts to protect the industrial arrival of the Northern Pacific Railroad to Bismarck, Dakota Territory. (SHSND.)

The soldiers above stood at attention, with band, facing to the southwest. The photograph dates to June 1877, one year after Custer fell at the Battle of Little Bighorn. (SHSND.)

Officers stationed at Fort Abraham Lincoln are within this photograph. From left to right are 2nd Lt. Charles A. Varnum (commander of Indian Scouts), Lieutenant Bronson, Cpt. Frederick W. Benteen, and 2nd Lt. Benjamin Hodgson (adjutant to Major Reno). Varnum and Benteen were wounded at Little Bighorn while Hodgson was killed. (NPS.)

Capt. Thomas Henry French (1843–1882) was a veteran of the Civil War and later stationed at Fort Abraham Lincoln. French's list of post–Civil War battles and expeditions included the Yellowstone Expedition (1873), the Battle of Little Big Horn (1876), and the Nez Perce Expedition (1877). In 1879, French was court martialed and dismissed from service for being drunk on duty, drinking with a laundress, and violating the terms of close arrest. (NPS.)

Charley Reynolds served as a guide for the 7th Cavalry. Reynolds served in the Civil War and later was stationed with the Union army at Fort Berthold from 1868 to 1872. He became a guide for the 7th Cavalry in 1873 and was killed during the Battle of the Little Bighorn. (NPS.)

This is a photograph of Pvt. John Burkman, Custer's striker. Strikers were enlisted soldiers who were servants for officers. Burkman sits in front of his tin shack near the railroad tracks in downtown Billings, Montana, shortly after the Battle of the Little Bighorn. With this photograph, he said, "Take me Mrs. Custer as I am. Your true servant John Burkman in my little home." Burkman took his own life not long after this photograph was taken. (NPS.)

This is a photograph of Dr. Benjamin Slaughter and his wife, Linda Slaughter, and family. Dr. Slaughter was a physician in the area of Fort Abraham Lincoln, stationed at Fort Rice (established 1864) to the south. Linda Slaughter served a short while as Camp Hancock's postmaster in the city of Bismarck across the Missouri River from Fort Abraham Lincoln. Linda Slaughter is the great-grandmother of North Dakota's 33rd governor, Doug Burgum. (SHSND.)

Frederick Frances Gerard (1823–1913) was an army scout for Custer and the 7th Cavalry. Gerard survived the Battle of Little Bighorn. He eventually married Ella S. Waddell and raised a family. The photographer was Orlando S. Goff, one of the primary photographers at Fort Abraham Lincoln. (SHSND.)

This is a portrait of Grant Prince Marsh, captain of the Far West, the steamboat that supplied the 7th Cavalry from Fort Abraham Lincoln to the Battle of Little Bighorn. On July 5, 1876, Marsh returned to Bismarck with the news of Custer's fall. Marsh communicated this information to Col. Clement Lounsberry of the *Bismarck Tribune*. Lounsberry wired this news to the *New York Herald*. From there, Custer's demise was communicated to the world. Marsh also served on steamboats with Mark Twain in 1858. Marsh died in 1916 and is buried in St. Mary's Cemetery, Bismarck. (SHSND.)

Sitting on the steps of the first commanding officer's quarters (the one that burned), from left to right, are (first row, sitting in front of Custer) Cpt. William Thompson; (second row) Elizabeth Custer, Lt. Col. George Custer, Fred Calhoun; (third row) Agnes Bates, Lt. James Calhoun, and Margaret Custer Calhoun. (SHSND.)

In this photograph, Custer and a group of cavalry officers and civilians stand next to two unidentified Indian Scouts. From left to right are Capt. William Winer Cooke, Emma Wadsworth, two Indian Scouts, Lieutenant Colonel Custer, Nellie Wadsworth, Tom Custer, Libby Custer, Mrs. Yates, and Lt. Winfield Scott Edgerly. Behind the group is the Missouri River. (NPS.)

This photograph of the Trader's Store at Fort Abraham Lincoln was taken sometime after 1886. Schlitz logos are visible within. North Dakota entered the Union as a dry state in 1889. This forced breweries, including the Milwaukee Brewery in the city of Bismarck across from Fort Abraham Lincoln, to close down. (SHSND.)

Custer and his sister, Margaret Custer Calhoun, are dressed as Quaker peace commissioners at Fort Abraham Lincoln. The photographer was Orlando Goff, and the photograph was taken in 1875. Pres. Ulysses S. Grant developed a Peace Policy during his administration, a controversial policy that moved between colonialism, paternalism, and forced assimilation. An alliance between Quakers and Episcopalians was attempted to help carry out this policy that eventually failed. (NPS.)

Seen here is another photograph of Custer and his sister, Margaret Calhoun, dressed as Quaker peace commissioners. Custer and Calhoun stand over Agnes Bates, sitting on the floor, who is representing the daughter of a northern Plains tribe's chief. Agnes and Elizabeth Custer remained friends after George Custer's death at the Battle of Little Bighorn/Greasy Grass. (NPS.)

This photograph of Lieutenant Colonel Custer shows him seated in his study with his wife, Elizabeth Bacon Custer, across from him. Seen here is a portrait of Custard (left), with a portrait of one of his former commanding officers, General McClellan (right). Portraits provided hosts with points of conversation when entertaining visitors. Custer would use these portraits to discuss his service with and for General McClellan during the Civil War. (NPS.)

This is a photograph of the parlor room in a commanding officer's quarters at Fort Abraham Lincoln. The group gathers around the piano to listen to playing and singing. Parlor rooms were also used to listen to readings and as a place to gather for conversation. (NPS.)

This photograph of Lieutenant Colonel Custer shows him reading in his study. Note the portrait of Custer hanging above him. A portrait of Civil War General McClellan is to the right, not visible. Behind Custer is a map of the Great Plains and American West. Fort Abraham Lincoln was one of several interconnected military forts throughout the northern Great Plains. (NPS.)

A group of surveyors are standing on the steps of the commanding officer's quarters at Fort Abraham Lincoln. Judging by the height of the leaves and branches in the top right and top left of this photograph, it was taken near the final years of Fort Abraham Lincoln in the late 1880s or early 1890s. (SHSND.)

Three

SCOUTS

This is an 1873 photograph of Bloody Knife, an Arikara who was a favorite scout of Custer. This photograph was taken during the Yellowstone Expedition of 1873. Three years later, Bloody Knife was killed during the Battle of Little Bighorn in June 1876. (NARA.)

Little Soldier was a Hunkpapa scout for Fort Abraham Lincoln and the United States. This photograph was taken on July 5, 1932, when he was 76 years old. (SHSND.)

Rain-in-the-Face was at the Battle of Little Bighorn/Greasy Grass and is recorded as killing Lt. Tom Custer, the younger brother of Lt. Col. George Custer. The inscription on the back of this original photograph reads, "Chief Rain-in-the-Face & Wife. From D.H. Barry [photographer]. To Mrs. Elizabeth B. Custer." (NPS.)

In 1873, Rain-in-the-Face took part in the Battle of Honsinger Bluff. In this battle, he killed army veterinarian Dr. John Hosinger. The Lakota attempted to defend their traditional lands from invaders in this way. The next year in 1874, Rain-in-the-Face was arrested by Lt. Tom Custer and imprisoned at Fort Abraham Lincoln for a short time. (NPS.)

Rain-in-the-Face was a major leader of the Lakota and fought against Custer and the 7th Cavalry at the Battle of Little Bighorn/Greasy Grass. (NPS.)

Here, Rain-in-the-Face is holding a repeater rifle. Cavalry of Fort Abraham Lincoln were outfitted with single shot carbines. The repeater rifle proved formative for the homeland forces of the combined tribes at the Battle of Little Bighorn/Greasy Grass. (NPS.)

Above is a lithograph of the Niimiipu. This indigenous nation was known as the Nez Perce to Europeans and Anglo-Americans. In 1877–1879, the Nez Perce, a tribe from the Pacific Northwest, were held as POWs at Fort Abraham Lincoln. Chief Joseph was among them. (SHSND.)

Blue Thunder, pictured here, was another Indian Scout for the United States at Fort Abraham Lincoln and Fort Rice. In 1874, Blue Thunder fought a three-day gun fight at the Little Heart Butte, 14 miles southwest of Fort Abraham Lincoln. (SHSND.)

Running Antelope was an Indian Scout for the United States on the northern Plains in the early 1880s. As a Scout, Running Antelope delivered mail between forts, including Fort Abraham Lincoln. (SHSND.)

Four

Steamboats and Horses

Before the construction of the Northern Pacific Railroad bridge across the Missouri River north of Fort Abraham Lincoln, the cable ferry was the dominant means of transportation across the river. During a few winters in the 1880s, temperatures were so cold that the Missouri River froze hard and thick enough to accommodate temporary Northern Pacific Railroad track being laid across it. (SHSND.)

This is a photograph of Dandy and Vic, two of Custer's horses when he was at Fort Abraham Lincoln. The caretaker is identified in the photograph as Burkman. (NPS.)

This winter photograph from 1875 shows a horse and sleigh ride at Fort Abraham Lincoln. Thomas Custer, William Cooke, and Agnes Wellington are in the sleigh. Custer and Cooke were killed in action on June 25, 1876, at the Battle of Little Bighorn. (NPS.)

Above is Capt. Thomas Weir's horse at Fort Abraham Lincoln in 1875. Captain Weir fought at the Battle of Little Bighorn. This campaign impaired his health, and he was reassigned from Fort Abraham Lincoln to the Cavalry Recruiting Office in New York City shortly after. (NPS.)

Another famous horse named Commanche (also spelled Comanche) stands above with the caretaker Pvt. Gustave Korn. Commanche was Captain Myles W. Koegh's horse at Fort Abraham Lincoln. Koegh was killed in action at the Battle of Little Bighorn while Commanche survived. Gustave Korn cared for Commanche after the Little Bighorn Battle. (NPS.)

This is another photograph of Commanche and Gustave Korn. This photograph would have been taken sometime before 1890, as Korn was killed at Wounded Knee on December 29, 1890. (NPS.)

This is a photograph of the steamboat *Far West*. The *Far West* and Capt. Grant Marsh supplied the 7th Cavalry during the campaign from Fort Abraham Lincoln to the Battle of Little Bighorn/Greasy Grass. Steamboats proved formative in extending the supply reach of colonizing powers throughout the 19th century. Today's Interstate 94 bridge that spans the Missouri River at Bismarck-Mandan is named Grant Marsh Bridge in honor of the Far West captain. (NDSU.)

This is a portrait of Capt. Grant Prince Marsh (1834–1916). Marsh served on riverboats with Mark Twain in 1858. In January 1916, Marsh passed away at St. Alexius Hospital (then at the corner of Sixth Street and Main Avenue in Bismarck) and is buried in St. Mary's Cemetery, Bismarck. (SHSND.)

Here is the Missouri River at Fort Abraham Lincoln in 1874. Note the log shacks on opposing banks of the river. The photographer is W.H. Illingworth, who accompanied Lieutenant Colonel Custer on the July 2 to August 30, 1874, expedition from Fort Abraham Lincoln to the Black Hills, southern Dakota Territory. A portion of the area they explored is today's Custer State Park in western South Dakota. (South Dakota State Historical Society.)

The steamboat *Denver* docked at Fort Abraham Lincoln during the summer of 1877. Frontier forts were often or exclusively located along navigable rivers so they could be supplied by steamboats. (SHSND.)

Five

1892 TO 1920S

Two years after North Dakota statehood in 1889, the United States decommissioned Fort Abraham Lincoln. Shortly after, nearby residents illegally disassembled the buildings and reused the lumber in their own construction projects. Pictured here is the dismantling of the commanding officer's quarters. (SHSND.)

Although a bit blurred, pictured here is the dismantling of officer's row, viewed from the south to the north. (SHSND.)

Locals, from one generation to the next, have remembered and memorialized Fort Abraham Lincoln and the personas attached to it in infinite ways. Here, an unidentified rider points to the ruins of the commanding officer's quarters at Fort Abraham Lincoln. (SHSND.)

This is a photograph of the site of the commanding officer's residence, with an unidentified individual standing nearby. This view is to the west. (SHSND.)

Handwritten on this photograph is the caption, "Hugo digging at S Eastern bank of 'Fort Lincoln' site A.D. 1904." The photographer is Ernest R. Steinbrueck (1833–1918) of Mandan, North Dakota. On June 3, 1904, Steinbrueck was appointed the first curator of collections of the State Historical Society of North Dakota (Bismarck). (SHSND.)

This photograph shows the top of the bluff where Fort McKeen was located. The image was dated 1905 and photographed by Steinbrueck, curator of the State Historical Society of North Dakota. Dr. Orin Libby, then the secretary of the State Historical Society of North Dakota, encouraged the documentation of the state's premier historic sites, including Fort Abraham Lincoln. (SHSND.)

The Mandan chapter of the Daughters of the American Revolution (DAR) installed a memorial at the site of Lieutenant Colonel Custer's last residence at Fort Abraham Lincoln. James W. Foley Jr., is next to the DAR sign in this photograph. Foley served as the *Bismarck Tribune*'s city editor in 1892 and went on to be the private secretary for North Dakota governor Elmore Yocum Sarles and North Dakota governor Louis Benjamin Hanna. Foley was eventually made poet laureate of North Dakota. (SHSND.)

Six

THE CIVILIAN CONSERVATION CORPS

From one generation to the next, local interest to reflect on and remember Fort Abraham Lincoln and the nationally important historical actors at the fort persisted since its establishment. Here is a view of the 60th anniversary of Custer and Fort Abraham Lincoln. (SHSND.)

Russell Reid, director of the State Historical Society of North Dakota, is pictured here. This photograph shows the method by which Reid would have photographed many of the CCC and National Park Service construction and memorialization efforts at Fort Abraham Lincoln State Park in the 1930s. (SHSND.)

In the 1930s, the blockhouses were reconstructed at the Fort McKeen infantry post that later became Fort Abraham Lincoln State Park. In the original 1870s Fort McKeen construction, the military also built a palisade wall. Within years, the palisade wall began to fail. When the CCC reconstructed this wall in the 1930s, they learned once again that it would fail within a couple years of construction. (SHSND.)

This is a view of the 1930s reconstructed fortification wall at historic Fort McKeen and the reconstructed blockhouses. This photograph would have been taken shortly after construction was completed. The Missouri River Valley is visible on the horizon in the distance of this photograph. (SHSND.)

This photograph was taken from the second story of the reconstructed blockhouse fortification at Fort McKeen. By following the fortification wall, the other two blockhouses are visible in the distance. (SHSND.)

This is a photograph of blockhouse reconstruction in the 1930s at historic Fort McKeen. This originally was an infantry post in the 1870s and was later subsumed with the establishment of Fort Abraham Lincoln. (SHSND.)

From its inception, the US Department of the Interior remained interested in Fort Abraham Lincoln; first as a cavalry post in the 1870s and later as developing it into a historic and recreational site in the 1930s. This is US Department of the Interior and National Park Service signage denoting the federal undertaking of construction and memorialization at Fort Abraham Lincoln State Park in the 1930s. (SHSND.)

This is a photograph of the 1930s memorial to the Custer Home. The inscription reads "CUSTER HOME, This was the site of the dwelling occupied by Gen. George A. Custer, Commanding Officer of Fort Abraham Lincoln from 1873 until his death at the battle of the Little Big Horn on June 25, 1876." (SHSND.)

During the infrastructure developments at Fort Abraham Lincoln in the 1930s, it was agreed upon that it was impractical to reconstruct every building as it once was in the 1870s. The main concern was how the state of North Dakota would maintain the infrastructure. Instead of building replicas of each structure, the CCC installed a series of corner markers at the approximate locations of the original 1870s buildings at Fort Abraham Lincoln. (SHSND.)

Here is additional signage from the 1930s, meant to inform visitors of locations of the 1870s barracks and blockhouses. (SHSND.)

This is another view of a large gathering in the 1930s at Fort Abraham Lincoln. Over 1,000-plus visitors are pictured in this image, a testament to the popularity of Fort Abraham Lincoln. (SHSND.)

This is a view of the earthlodge reconstruction from the 1930s at On-A-Slant Village. This view is from the hilltop of historic Fort McKeen. In the distance the cottonwood trees can be seen reflecting off the water from the Missouri River. Below the Missouri River, the Heart River is visible. (SHSND.)

This is a 1932 aerial view of On-A-Slant Village. The Heart River is visible just above the village in this photo, and the Missouri River Valley is above that. (SHSND.)

In this photograph, excavation work is underway in the 1930s. Excavation work revealed details about the fortification ditch and palisade wall surrounding the traditional Mandan village, and details of earthlodge locations. (SHSND.)

Russell Reid photographed the excavation crew at On-A-Slant Village in 1934. Power lines are also seen mid-right in the photo. Providing electricity to the rural areas of the Great Plains and the United States was another large, federal undertaking, spearheaded in cooperation with rural electric cooperatives. On May 11, 1935, Pres. Franklin Roosevelt issued Executive Order 7037, which created the Rural Electrification Administration. The next year, the US Congress passed the Rural Electrification Act of 1936. Rural electrification helped modernize the United States so that it could more effectively compete on the world stage. (SHSND.)

Local timber was harvested during the 1930s CCC and National Park Service construction projects at Fort Abraham Lincoln. Two wood cutters are seen here felling a tree. (SHSND.)

This photograph shows continued tree felling for building earthlodges at Fort Abraham Lincoln in the 1930s. (SHSND.)

This is another tree felling photograph for construction projects at Fort Abraham Lincoln. One logger looks on as two other loggers saw the trunk of this tree. (SHSND.)

Two laborers saw while one looks on with a long ax wedge. The snow in the photograph gives an idea as to the time of the year that the loggers worked to get the timbers cut and prepared to stage for earthlodge construction. (SHSND.)

Six laborers lift a large timber. The slogan of the Civilian Conservation Corps was "We can take it!" The CCC program included work, calisthenics, marching drill, good food and medical care. (SHSND.)

Two laborers saw while a third photographs. The photographer's shadow is visible in the photo. The CCC allowed for male, unmarried laborers ages 18 to 25 initially, and eventually ages 17 to 28. (SHSND.)

Timbers were transported by truck from where they were felled to the construction location. (SHSND.)

Before actual construction could commence, the staging of materials, including logs, was required. The Heart River confluence at the Missouri River is visible top-right. The Missouri River can be seen winding back and forth in the distance toward the horizon. (SHSND.)

This is a photograph of earthlodge construction progress. A truck is visible in the photograph, along with laborers. This helps the viewer understand the scale of the size of the CCC earthlodges. (SHSND.)

Here are staged materials for earthlodge construction. After the trees were felled, they were stripped of bark and staged in front of the earthlodge locations. (SHSND.)

Logs are staged for earthlodge construction. Poles and pulleys are visible in the background. Cottonwood trees are common along the Missouri River bottoms on the northern Plains. Cottonwood trees were utilized for centuries by the Mandan and Hidatsa peoples for infrastructure needs. The Mandan and Hidatsa built an extensive system of villages with cottonwood trees up and down the Missouri River in central North Dakota. (SHSND.)

A system of pulleys were used to lift the large timbers during earthlodge construction. The CCC workers used trucks and modern mechanized equipment to build the earthlodges in the 1930s. The Mandan people, however, would have built earthlodges and entire villages without equipment afforded by the industrial revolution of the 19th century. (SHSND.)

This is a view of the construction progress from inside the earthlodge. In the background is the butte where historic Fort McKeen was established in the 1870s. (SHSND.)

More timbers are being set into place above. These timbers would provide the foundational structure of the layers of willow branches, woven grass thatching, clay, and soil to complete the earthlodge construction. (SHSND.)

Here horizontal thatching is layered on the earthlodge timbers. (SHSND.)

The CCC also used metal saws and axes during earthlodge construction. The traditional construction of these earthlodges would have been completed with stone and bone tools. (SHSND.)

This photograph shows the clay and soil that are layered on top of the horizontal grass thatching. The earthlodge entrance is middle-right in this photo. (SHSND.)

Work trucks near the earthlodges provide scale and perspective of earth lodge size. This photograph is of near completion of the reconstructed earthlodges. The earthlodge materials allowed for them to remain cool during the summer. In the winter, through human, domestic animal, and fireside heat, the earthlodges remained warm. (SHSND.)

Here, CCC workers construct the foundation of the bridge base that leads from the museum to On-A-Slant Village. The stone used was local, and shaped and cut on site by the CCC. (SHSND.)

Pictured is continued progress of the bridge substructure. (SHSND.)

Cut stone was slid down a chute before it was moved into position and set. (SHSND.)

Laborers stand on top of the substructure and receive mortar from a chute delivered to them from the workers above. (SHSND.)

The finished stone and timber bridge spans the natural valley between the museum and village site. This design became a distinct architectural style known as WPA Rustic. (SHSND.)

This bridge spanned the ravine between the CCC museum and the earthlodge reconstructions. During the time the village was occupied in the 18th century and prior, this valley acted as a natural defensive barrier. (SHSND.)

The CCC infrastructure has lasted for decades at Fort Abraham Lincoln. This CCC project was one of hundreds throughout the United States in the 1930s. Much of the infrastructure was so well built that it continues to be in use well into the 21st century. (SHSND.)

The CCC was trained and directed to bring about conservation within the projects. This was a result of the Dust Bowl that dominated the Great Plains. Industrial farming plowed up native grasses and prairie, and this led to the Dust Bowl. The CCC was developed to respond to this. (SHSND.)

Above is a close-up photograph of the CCC steps after installation. (SHSND.)

Here is the completed CCC bridge with steps leading to On-A-Slant Village. This heavy lift of 1930s CCC infrastructure was a testament to how well appreciated Fort Abraham Lincoln and the adjoining On-A-Slant Village was from one generation to the next. (SHSND.)

Foundational forms begin to take shape with the construction of the concession building. The forms are in place and ready to receive concrete just east of the main museum. Today, a thick grove of trees surrounds this grouping of CCC buildings. (SHSND.)

The CCC was deliberate in construction methods and techniques. Because of this, the CCC buildings remain in use today throughout city, county, state, and federal parks in the United States. Here is a cross section of those 1930s construction techniques, with the continued work on raising the walls. (SHSND.)

This photograph reflects the onsite stone cutting and setting of the stones to raise the walls of the museum and outbuildings. Drill marks are visible in the stone block closest in this image. (SHSND.)

Five CCC laborers continue setting one layer of cut stone after another. The portico is becoming visible in this image. This building in the 21st century is surrounded by a grove of trees to the north and east and a parking lot to the south. (SHSND.)

This is a photograph of the completed building that served as a place for preparing, selling, and serving concessions at Fort Abraham Lincoln State Park. (SHSND.)

This photograph shows the completed concessions building before the landscaping was finished. An earthlodge is visible in the distance, center left in the photograph. (SHSND.)

A photograph of the completed concessions building with the view facing the Missouri River to the east. The patio installation is underway in the photograph. (SHSND.)

This photograph is a view to the north of the completed museum building's south elevation. One of the three reconstructed Fort McKeen blockhouses is visible on the bluff to the left of the museum. In modern times, the growth of the trees around the museum block this view of the 1930s. (SHSND.)

This is a photograph of the raising of the museum entrance wall. The walls were built of local granite and large timber framing. This is one of the defining features of the Rustic WPA architectural style in North Dakota. (SHSND.)

This is a view of the masonry arch museum entrance that consists of 12 granite blocks plus a centered keystone. (SHSND.)

Pulleys and levers were used to move blocks into place and set them. A system of wood scaffolding was also built so workers could rise alongside the wall. (SHSND.)

Stone cutters and masons are center left in this photograph. The CCC was a program that would put laborers to work, with opportunities for the laborers to train and become skilled workers. (SHSND.)

This is a photograph of eight CCC laborers cutting and preparing stone blocks that would be installed in the walls of the museum building. (SHSND.)

The heavy garments suggest that the work is taking place on a cold North Dakota winter day. (SHSND.)

A large stone inscribed with "State Historical Society 1936" is being set in place. The State Historical Society of North Dakota, specifically Dr. Orin G. Libby, the first professional historian in the state of North Dakota, took an early interest in Fort Abraham Lincoln as an historic site with regional and national importance. Dr. Libby received his PhD from the University of Wisconsin under the direction of Frederick Jackson Turner, the "father" of American History. (SHSND.)

The "State Historical Society 1936" stone is being lowered into place. A bit of ceremony took place with the setting of this stone. A group of onlookers are visible behind the two individuals setting the stone. (SHSND.)

The "State Historical Society 1936" stone is set into place with a system of pulleys and chain. Because of the historical significance of Fort Abraham Lincoln State Park, before it became a state park it was largely overseen and cared for by the State Historical Society of North Dakota. Russell Reid and Dr. Orin Libby indeed understood the significance and importance of this fort in local, state and national history. (SHSND.)

This is a photograph of the crowd assembled for the setting of the "State Historical Society 1936" stone. (SHSND.)

Above is a photograph of the completed stone arched entrance, with the "State Historical Society 1936" cornerstone block visible bottom left, and the CCC system of scaffolding situated center left. A scattering of stone cuttings is at the bottom right of this photograph. (SHSND.)

The scaffolding structure protected workers and materials from the elements, with a stovepipe and canvas curtains also visible. The upper tier of scaffolding was heated. (SHSND.)

This is the view down one of the sections of the museum wall, with masonry string and lag bolts visible. (SHSND.)

This photograph of the completed museum and concession building captures the southwest elevation. (SHSND.)

Approximately 20 CCC laborers are in this photograph, near to far. After the completion of the stone walkway, the installation of sod clumps commenced. On a national level, it was common for the CCC to undertake soil conservation projects, including this one. The goal of soil conservation projects was to inhibit and thwart another Dust Bowl, an event that swept nutrient rich soil from the agricultural fields of the Great Plains. Without these soils, farmers and ranchers would lose the most important resource of their lands. (SHSND.)

In this photograph, CCC laborers within the museum entrance frame up partition walls. To the right, another group of CCC laborers leverage the stone walkway into place, one stone at a time. (SHSND.)

With the completed museum in the forefront of this photograph, the reconstructed earthlodges are visible mid-right. Russell Reid would have taken this photograph. Reid was a longtime friend of George Will, a Bismarck native and Harvard trained archaeologist who excavated the Double Ditch State Historic Site north of Bismarck. George Will's residence is in Bismarck's historic Cathedral District today. (SHSND.)

In this photographic overview of the complex of CCC buildings, to the right is the museum, the administrative outbuilding is to the left, and the concession building is above. In the distance, the Missouri River sweeps left to right across the photograph, not too far below the horizon. (SHSND.)

In the foreground, CCC laborers work at installing the foundation of what would become the entrance sign. In the background, just in front of the museum, additional CCC laborers continue with the landscaping. (SHSND.)

The CCC is installing the entrance sign in this photograph. The sign reads, "Museum, Concessions, Parking." (SHSND.)

This is a photograph of another view of the "Museum, Concessions, Parking" sign. A concrete and mortar-mixing drum is center left. The CCC projects tended to emphasize the overbuilt, as the design and construction were meant to last for generations. (SHSND.)

This photograph shows the completed "Museum, Concession, Parking" sign. This sign was immediate to the automotive trail that wound through the recreational park and historic site. (SHSND.)

Construction began on the entrance sign at the state historic recreational site. (SHSND.)

Completed markers were installed by the CCC that denoted Fort (Abraham) Lincoln and a sign that directed visitors to the museum and concessions buildings. At the time of this 1930s construction, Fort Abraham Lincoln's establishment as a military fort on the Missouri River was just over 60 years old. (SHSND.)

The CCC installed directional signs for the nationally important Fort Abraham Lincoln historic site. The signs included directions for park visitors. A shed roof lean-to is visible center left. (SHSND.)

Just below the butte where Fort McKeen was established in the 1870s, CCC laborers begin the foundational work of a shelter in the 1930s. (SHSND.)

The CCC installed a stone perimeter along the pedestrian and automotive trails. There are wide wood mallet hand tools visible, used for tamping and leveling the soil prior to installing the heavy cut stones. (SHSND.)

Here is another photograph of a CCC designed and built pedestrian walkway and stone perimeter wall. The leveling string is visible in this photograph. (SHSND.)

The CCC utilized stone landscaping to define the automotive trails throughout the park. Since the rise of the automobile through the mass-produced assembly line, automobiles became more and more affordable throughout the United States. A result of this was an increase in automobile touring. The National Park Service, and the automobile manufacturers, encouraged this automotive touring throughout the system of parks. Infrastructure was built to accommodate them. (SHSND.)

This photograph shows the view toward the Missouri River of the construction entrance driveway to the concessions and museum parking lot. In the distance, CCC laborers continue to set stone. (SHSND.)

A CCC laborer stands on top of a completed section of stone patio. The CCC, a public work relief program created to counter the Great Depression and help mitigate the economic anxieties of the nation, accepted unmarried male laborers initially from the ages of 18–25 but later expanded to 17–28. (SHSND.)

CCC laborers pump water from a well near a road that ascends to historic Fort McKeen. (SHSND.)

This close-up view of the corner floor of a shelter was just below the bluff of historic Fort McKeen. (SHSND.)

This detailed photograph shows how the rafters and beams of the picnic shelter were assembled by CCC laborers. (SHSND.)

This view faces the river to the southeast. This CCC style—prairie fieldstones topped with large timber rafter framing—was a defining feature of CCC architecture throughout North Dakota's system of state and county parks. Today, because of this CCC architectural style from the 1930s and the heavy scholarly lifting of Steve Martens (North Dakota State University emeritus professor of Architecture), this architectural style is eligible for the National Register of Historic Places. (SHSND.)

In this photograph, four CCC laborers set rafter logs into position and bring the WPA Rustic architectural style into focus. The logs required on-site notching before they were set into place. (SHSND.)

Several CCC laborers stand on top of the shelter construction in this photograph. At the top left, one CCC laborer continues to notch a large log with an ax. (SHSND.)

Before the installation of the roof shakes, the roofing cross members were set into place to receive the roof sheathing. Just over the horizon center left, one of the CCC Fort McKeen reconstructed blockhouses is visible. (SHSND.)

This is another view of the picnic shelter before it received a shake roof. The walls of CCC WPA Rustic–style construction has stood the test of time, while roofing and rafters have required replacement. (SHSND.)

The completed shelter had irregular sized local granite fieldstones and irregular course layers that characterize the WPA Rustic architectural style. (Both, SHSND.)

Pictured above is another angle of the completed shelter. The photographic documentation captured images of the WPA Rustic architecture in its original, finished form. (SHSND.)

The surrounding area was landscaped and finished in this view of the shelter. The road behind the shelter leads up to historic Fort McKeen. (SHSND.)

The CCC built restrooms at Fort Abraham Lincoln for recreational uses. In this photograph, a CCC laborer puts the finishing touches on the shake roof. (SHSND.)

A CCC laborer finished the roof crown with cedar shakes. (SHSND.)

Here are the completed log cabin restrooms at Fort Abraham Lincoln. A sign to the left of the restroom entryway says, "Women." (SHSND.)

In this photograph of the completed log cabin restrooms, the sign at the right of the entryway indicates it is the entrance for the "Men." (SHSND.)

A CCC laborer continues to finish the installation of the cedar shakes on the roof of the log cabin restrooms. (SHSND.)

This stairway ascended to the restrooms at Fort Abraham Lincoln. (SHSND.)

The initiative of the Civilian Conservation Corps was nationwide, with 52 camps in North Dakota. It was CCC Camp SP-3 No. 2775-V that was stationed one mile south of Mandan at Fort Abraham Lincoln. This 1938 photograph shows a dike that surrounds the camp buildings. The photographer is identified as Russell Reid from the State Historical Society of North Dakota. Reid would eventually go on to become the director of the State Historical Society of North Dakota. (SHSND.)

Throughout the 1920s, the North Dakota Highway Department had established campaigns that encouraged automotive touring of heritage and recreational sites. To meet the needs of this automotive tourism, resources were directed to help heritage sites built impressive infrastructure to accommodate the increase in traffic. The impressive infrastructure was intended to leave a lasting impression in the minds of the visitors, thereby enticing them to return and tell others about the wonders of the site. Here, heritage tourists and visitors are parked in front of the CCC museum in the newly constructed automotive parking lot. (SHSND.)

Seven

The 1960s Custer Drama

The Custer Drama was played out at Fort Abraham Lincoln from 1959 through 1968. This is a photograph from one of the scenes. The Mandan Historical Society, in their online write up of *The Custer Drama*, has noted the following: "The original production [of the *Custer Drama*] called 'Trail West' was written by W.T. Chichester and Frederick G. Walsh. Walsh was instrumental in starting operations at the Burning Hills Amphitheater in Medora, ND with his drama 'Old Four Eyes' highlighting the life of Theodore Roosevelt. This production was the predecessor to the 'Medora Musical' which continues in production today." Since the Battle of Little Bighorn in 1876, the remembrance of Custer has been revisited and reinterpreted in infinite ways. In this regard, the way that Custer is remembered throughout time can be used to as a social barometer. (SHSND.)

The character playing Custer signals to the 7th Cavalry to advance and move forward. The actor playing Custer wears buckskins, a part of the unconventional clothing that Custer himself wore during his lifetime. Since the time he served as a Union officer during the American Civil War, and his post–Civil War period on the Great Plains and American West, Custer often dressed in clothing to make himself distinguished from the rank and file. Officers dressing uniquely such as this was not uncommon, though. It served a purpose, as enlisted soldiers and cavalry could better identify their commanding officers in the field of battle. Considering the size and scale of armies in the second half of the 19th century, winning and losing battles depended on clear communication between officers and the soldiers they led. (SHSND.)

This photograph is a view from atop the bluff of *The Custer Drama.* The Mandan Historical Society has noted that *The Custer Drama* lasted from 1959 to 1968. Casting tryouts were held every spring to fill the roles of 80 cast members. The amphitheater had seating for 2,000, and the 110-foot stage ran shows from July 1 through Labor Day with performances each day from Wednesday through Sunday. Cast members came from as far away as Duluth, Minnesota, and Chicago, Illinois. (SHSND.)

The actor Custer gestures to the cavalry behind him. From 1959 to 1968, *The Custer Drama* was played out at the Custer Memorial Amphitheater at Fort Abraham Lincoln. The year 1962 commemorated the centennial establishment of Dakota Territory, which was created under the auspices of Pres. Abraham Lincoln during the American Civil War. (SHSND.)

The actor Custer grasps the hand of the unidentified actress playing Custer's wife, Elizabeth "Libby" Bacon Custer. Promoting historical figures as "larger than life" has been a central driver in the promotion of heritage tourism throughout the state of North Dakota. (SHSND.)

The Custer Drama cast members act out a scene, with soldiers of the 7th Cavalry and laundresses cheering on two cavalry actors. (SHSND.)

The actor Custer gestures with a pointed finger and a stern look. In 1958, the City of Mandan's chamber of commerce approached Frederick G. Walsh to draft a play for use at Fort Abraham Lincoln. The Mandan Historical Society has noted that the "drama boasted the distinction of being located on the exact trail used by General Custer and the men as they left the Fort on May 17, 1876." (SHSND.)

The actor Custer reads a newspaper, with a map of Dakota Territory and the Big Horn River behind him. The natural waterways of the northern intermountain American West are also featured on this map. These waterways provided steamboats with a route and the ability to supply and resupply military expeditions. (SHSND.)

The actor playing George Custer and the actress Libby Custer are shown here on stage at the dinner table. (SHSND.)

The actor Custer gestures to the actresses, presumably departing for the last time from Fort Abraham Lincoln for the Little Bighorn. (SHSND.)

In the 1960s production of *The Custer Drama*, the actor Custer salutes the others from his horse. (SHSND.)

Cavalry actors ride through the gates of the Fort Abraham Lincoln stage. The stage walls in this photograph do not accurately represent Fort Abraham Lincoln, as the original Fort Abraham Lincoln was not surrounded by fortification walls. However, the walls in this photograph provided a backdrop and setting for the stage. (SHSND.)

The actor Custer addresses his enlisted cavalry on stage. (SHSND.)

The actor Custer is surrounded by four of the 7th Cavalry that he would have led. (SHSND.)

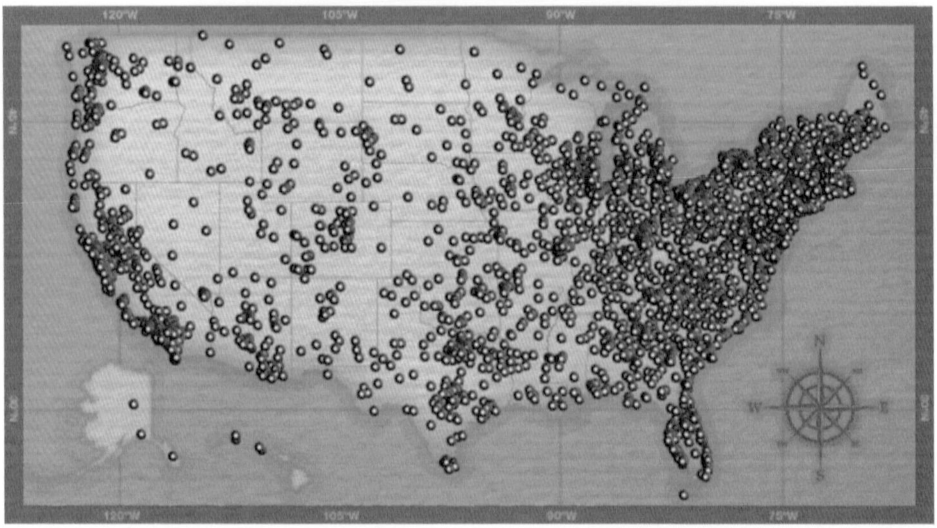